The Confident Presenter

A Handbook For Beginning Speakers

By

Ryan P. Hall

This book is a work of fiction. Places, events, and situations in this story are purely fictional. Any resemblance to actual persons, living or dead, is coincidental.

© 2003 by Ryan P. Hall. All rights reserved.

No part of this book may be reproduced, stored in a retrieval system, or transmitted by any means, electronic, mechanical, photocopying, recording, or otherwise, without written permission from the author.

ISBN: 1-4107-6043-X (e-book)
ISBN: 1-4107-6044-8 (Paperback)

Library of Congress Control Number: 2003093551

This book is printed on acid free paper.

Printed in the United States of America
Bloomington, IN

1stBooks - rev. 6/30/03

This book is inspired by all of the wonderful Miami and Antonelli students I have had the pleasure of teaching in the past, and all of the colleagues I have had the pleasure of working with. May you have learned from me as much as I have learned from you.

I would like to thank Mary Ann Davis, Jim Slouffman, and Karen Selby for their support of this project.

This book is dedicated to my wife Stephanie. Her encouragement and belief in me were the impetus for this project.

Table Of Contents

Introduction

Advice From One Presenter To Another

"You have a speech due next Friday." Those seven words, uttered by any speech instructor, in any classroom, in any part of the world can turn confident and proud individuals into nervous, and even angry, beings. Being a speech instructor for both a large university and a well-respected two-year college, I have seen the unfortunate consequences of uttering those seven words, or any variation thereof. I have seen the fear in the eyes of the students. I have felt the stifling tension within the air. I have heard the nervous laughter from the back of the room. I have seen students cry on speech day. I have had a student run out of the class, in the *middle* of her speech. Not surprisingly, I have had students, with previous good health and attendance, mysteriously absent on the day their speech was due.

It is for these reasons that I write this handbook on speaking effectiveness. I fully empathize with those individuals who cannot stand speaking in public, or those who are uncomfortable with speaking in public because they feel they do not know how to construct a well-organized, audience-oriented speech.

I felt those same uneasy feelings prior to a speech, for as long as I can remember. I would feel sick to my stomach while my throat seemed to tighten up. Not only did I feel nauseous in my stomach, but I also felt a lump in my throat, which I felt would make me physically sick. I would somehow find the courage to walk up to the front of the classroom, and begin my speech, a speech that I would read straight off of my note cards, not looking at the audience once. As I clutched my note cards, I would zip through my words, and then hurry back to my seat, thankful my speech was over.

I knew, however, that I could not allow myself to speak like this forever. I would come to understand that almost everybody felt nervous about speaking, yet those who excelled in speaking seemed to posses the ability to *influence* the people around them. By influence, I mean the intangible quality to relax an audience, encourage them to believe in you, and sometimes, get the audience to do what you want them to do. I know this may seem grandiose, but think about someone you admire. They probably have the ability to communicate effectively, while not alienating themselves or others. The ability to influence others, whether it is in a public speaking setting, or everyday conversation, is one of the keys to advancing your career. Politicians (whether we like them or not), CEO's, instructors, members of the clergy, community leaders, certain sports figures (ever wonder why some sports icons are in so many commercials and others are disliked by the media?) all possess the ability to influence others.

The one surefire way to influence others is through your voice and actions. We, as human beings, have the ability to soothe hurt feelings, or crush fragile confidences. It's our choice how we use our voice. Public speaking can help us practice our influential voice and appropriate nonverbal delivery for when we need to put it into action. The more practice we undertake in the public speaking setting the more comfortable we will be in diverse speaking situations; whether those situations are a salary negotiation with your employer or a sales presentation to a client.

I have overcome my abject fear of public speaking and feel the insights that I have learned, along with the years of teaching collegiate public speaking courses will benefit the beginning speaker. The material in this book will focus only on the beginning stages of speaking development: overcoming stage fright, speaking with the audience's needs in mind, organizing main points, effectively beginning and ending main points, types of organizational patterns, delivery effectiveness, supporting material and visual aids. After a speaker masters these skills, then and only then can they progress on to persuasion and other advanced forms of public speaking (such as impromptu speaking and debates). A speaker should not try to tackle advanced forms of speaking without mastering the beginning stages first because a weak grasp of foundational skills will only lead to weaker applications of more advanced skills. This same logic applies in mathematics: we should never place a math student in a calculus class if he/she cannot fully grasp the material in their algebra class.

The advice in the ensuing pages has evolved through the experiences of the countless presentations and seminars that I have delivered, and the public speaking classes that I have taught. These experiences can give you a realistic approach to public speaking success. I am grateful you chose to take the first few steps of your public speaking journey with me. May the advice you read provide you with the knowledge you seek to help you achieve the success you want.

Immutable-not capable of or susceptible to change;
from Latin *immutabilis*

Chapter 1

The Importance Of Public Speaking

"The public is the only critic whose opinion is worth anything at all."
Mark Twain

Immutable Truth #1:

People enjoy being around well-spoken, intelligent individuals. People avoid abrasive, disrespectful individuals. How you are perceived by others is largely up to you.

At the beginning of every term, I review the course syllabus and expectations, and allow time for students to ask questions about the course. Once in a while, I hear something along the lines of, "I am afraid of public speaking. I don't know if I ever will have to give presentations after graduation. Why do they make us take this class anyway?" Students generally want to know why they are being subjected to a high-stress class, and what is in it for them.

This curiosity is well founded, and I feel it necessary to address these concerns at the outset of this book. This chapter will detail the advantages of becoming a polished public speaker, public speaking situations you may encounter and how public speaking is a celebration of democracy and the human spirit.

ADVANTAGES OF BEING A POLISHED PUBLIC SPEAKER

Could you imagine a world without conversations, songs telephone calls, T.V. shows, movies, and negotiations? What a bland existence and world it would be! We use our voice to our advantage everyday, and without our voice human evolution would only be stagnant. Being a polished public speaker has many advantages to both you, and the world around you. Let's look at four such advantages:

- Being a polished speaker means you have learned a lot about the practice of speaking. Consequently, you will become **CONFIDENT** in your beliefs and words. You will come to look forward to speaking engagements, as you will see those engagements as a chance to showcase your knowledge and skills. Further, you will not hesitate to speak up in your personal and professional life, because you will have thought out your ideas and arguments in an intelligent manner. Being confident in your voice and not worrying about your public speaking fears will allow you to focus and improve on other aspects of your personal and/or professional duties.

- Taking the speaking stage with confidence will allow you to maximize your ability to **INFLUENCE** your audience. Do you want to succeed at sales presentations? How about job interviews? Employers seek candidates who can adequately describe their qualifications. The extent to which you relate your qualifications to the employer's needs will go a long way toward your interviewing success. Do you feel passionately about something within your community? Using your voice at rallies and open-forums can greatly benefit your ability to influence your peers and decision-makers.
- As a result of being able to influence those around you, a polished speaker can initiate **CHANGE** for the greater good. Do you feel a policy at work needs to be rewritten in order to clarify and update business issues? What if you disagree with a performance review you received from a superior? How do you communicate this disagreement with tact and professionalism? How do you go about getting back into his/her good graces? There will be times you have to take a stand for something, which may result in you meeting resistance from others. The chances of you being able to negotiate your way through this resistance, in order to bring about positive change is greatly increased if you can articulate your feelings in accordance with the views of others.

- A well-spoken individual can be perceived by others as being **CREDIBLE**; that is the extent to which people believe and trust you. Trustworthiness is a very important quality in today's dynamic and fast-paced society. If a customer is dissatisfied with service, he/she can go to a competitor rather easily, never to return to do business with you again. However, if the customer genuinely believes that you are concerned about his/her problem and the actions you will take to ameliorate the situation, perhaps he/she will continue to do business with you. If you fail to build credibility with your co-workers and boss, they may not trust you with important tasks and assignments. Not a big deal, you say? Think about it like this—if you are not working on important assignments, how important is it for your company to give you a nice raise? How important is it for your company to keep you around?

These advantages are just the tip of the iceberg. Learning how to speak well in public can also help you think on your feet, and remain calm when audience members become listless or disrespectful in presentations. Also, you can better overcome buyer objections if you can maximize your thoughts and tap into their needs. The cost of not speaking well in public could just be your lack of career advancement and consequently, your financial outlook.

PUBLIC SPEAKING SITUATIONS YOU MAY ENCOUNTER

As stated earlier, we use our voice daily and in many diverse situations. You can help yourself or hurt yourself in these situations, depending on how you use your voice. Here are just a few situations in which we use our voice to help ourselves:

- Professional networking functions
- Client/Customer relationships
- Vendor negotiations
- Job interviews
- Sales presentations and buyer objections
- Stating your view on why you think your department needs twenty computers when management is only willing to purchase fifteen
- Home Owner Association meetings
- School Board meetings
- Community issues and other public forums

Again, the list can go on for quite some time. Due to the increased competition by our competitors and our fast paced culture, it is imperative we make the most of our speaking voice in these situations. Also, look at it from another point of view: an employer will be looking for someone who is articulate and professional, and the employer will base some of this judgment on how well the candidate speaks. Who would you hire? Someone who is disrespectful, becomes flustered easily, or cannot develop ideas fully? Or, perhaps someone who is focused on the moment and can articulate his/her thoughts well in relation to that moment. The same holds true for clients. They want to work with someone who is approachable, knowledgeable, and respectful. How else could you convey those traits than through how you speak? Remember, that clients (and employers for that matter) buy into you first before they buy into your work.

PUBLIC SPEAKING IS A CELEBRATION OF DEMOCRACY AND HUMAN SPIRIT

Our country was founded because a change was needed in the lives of the colonists, and the colonists used their voice to construct a new country. When the Bill of Rights was ratified on December 15, 1791, it encouraged the freedom of speech for all U.S. citizens, recognizing the importance of differing views and ideas as necessary for the growth of democracy. Using your voice is what this country was founded on, and is just as important now as it was back in the 18th century. The belief that no matter your age, your gender, your race, your nationality, or your ethnic class, you have the ability to speak your mind, convey your thoughts, and become an agent of change as much or as little as you'd like is a great compliment to the human race.

Further, using your voice and speaking in public can lead to **NOBLE** outcomes (characterized by, or arising from superiority of mind or character or of ideals or morals). You can speak on behalf of those you care for and/or those who cannot speak for themselves. How many lives have been improved because someone championed a cause and saw an issue through to resolution? I bet the following individuals have:

- Social workers
- Peace negotiators
- Animal welfare officers
- Attorneys
- Judges
- Managers and other noble leaders
- Mediators
- Union representatives
- City Council members
- Senators and other members of the government
- Parents and grandparents; siblings
- Members of the clergy

Indeed, we can use our voice to bring about improved situations not only for ourselves, but others. It may sound extravagant, but may not be too far off to say that through your voice you can positively influence the human spirit!

So, why do you think it is important to learn how to speak well in public? You owe it to the betterment of yourself and those around you. It is that simple.

"There is only one corner of the universe you can be certain of improving, and that's your own self."

Aldous Huxley

CHAPTER REFLECTION

1. Based on your goals and motivations, how can improving your public speaking ability help you?

2. Can you think of a time when someone used his/her voice to help you out of a potential problem? Reflect on the situation below.

3. Seek out a person who works in the professional field in which you want to work or learn more about. Ask them how important it is to have good communication skills (to read people, speak in public, handle difficult people, close sales deals…), and reflect on their answers below.

Chapter 2

Public Speaking Fears

"Nothing is so much to be feared as fear."

Henry David Thoreau

Immutable Truth #2:

It is okay to feel uneasy about speaking in public; however, the only way to overcome feelings of uneasiness is to practice speaking well in front of others, and reflecting on what you can do to improve from each time to the next. Period.

Nothing evokes panic and feelings of fear more than the thought of having to give a speech, and it may not matter who the audience is. Confident people, who have no problem sharing opinions and ideas suddenly "clam up," while others turn red and feel as if they will faint. As a speech teacher, I have seen all sorts of reactions, and believe me when I say this: I can totally sympathize. It was not that long ago that I was frightened with the mere notion of just participating in class discussions, let alone giving a five minute informative speech. Yikes, indeed!

Fortunately, through practice and determination, I was able to overcome my public speaking fears, and now I share my insights with my public speaking classes. I see the angst they go through and truly feel that every one of them can eventually get to the point where they see their public speaking as not only easy, but also an asset to their career advancement. This chapter will explore why speakers fear speaking in public, ways to overcome speech apprehension, and the costs associated with letting fear of public speaking control your speaking experiences.

WHY PUBLIC SPEAKING IS INTIMIDATING

First, let me say again that most, if not all, people experience some form of stage fright—that is physical or mental discomfort associated with speaking in front of other people. Hot flashes, feeling sick to your stomach, sweaty palms, shortness of breath, and dry mouth are all symptoms of stage fright. I find it odd that even though most people are of adequate to high intelligence, they are mortally afraid to share their views (and sometimes these views are needed to be heard) in a public format. Why is speaking in front of others so frightening?

Through the years, I have asked and formally surveyed my classes on their thoughts as to why public speaking is so frightening. Some of the more consistent responses are listed here:

- "People can see you mess up—you are the center of attention."
- "It is more the fear of being made fun of by saying the wrong thing or looking nervous."
- "Speaking in public is frightening for me because I fear that I will be judged—not in a positive light."
- "Speaking in public is frightening because many people feel like their ideas/opinions will not be accepted by others. They do not like everyone staring at them or analyzing them. It puts them out in the open when they would rather keep their ideas/feelings to themselves."
- "For me, public speaking is so frightening because I'm leaving myself open for judgment. I'm not confident enough in my speech writing ability to share it with everyone."

These responses are consistent throughout my classes and throughout the years. It begins to make sense to me: people fear speaking in public because they are not *used* to doing it. Usually, we do not like to focus on our shortcomings; what we are not so good at. We like to stay in our comfort zones, and speaking in public is certainly not in our zone of comfort. Combine these notions with the idea that we may be evaluated on what we say, and how we say it, you then have a less-than-desirable situation afoot.

I can compare this uneasiness to the first time I rode my bike—I fell off and banged up my shins. Not only did my shins ache, but I also had a bruised ego because I tried to do something and failed at it. I did not want to continue to ride my bike anymore. However, I knew that if I wanted to hang out with the other kids in the neighborhood who could ride their bikes, I would have to learn. I could not become better at riding my bike by watching the other kids ride theirs; I couldn't get better by reading about how to ride a bike effectively. So, through practice and diligence, I finally learned how to ride my bike, and as you probably know, riding a bike now is never the stressful experience it once was.

Speaking in public is much the same as learning to ride your bike; painful, embarrassing at times, and awkward. However, once you get the hang of both, they are quite easy and both are very rewarding. In order to become more comfortable with speaking in public you have to practice a ton, and learn from each speaking experience. Just like riding a bike, you have to do it.

OVERCOMING OUR FEAR OF PUBLIC SPEAKING

The best way beginning speakers can overcome their fear of public speaking is to **speak more and not avoid it**. However, I feel the speaker's mindset has to be focused on learning how to speak effectively and not just going through the motions. So much of life is how we perceive it—we can choose to be a victim of our situation or we can choose to take control of a situation. We can choose to get angry at traffic (and it is easy to do!), or we can choose to not let it affect us. Further, we can choose to learn to go another route or leave ten minutes earlier, thus avoiding the traffic altogether. Sometimes, working smarter and not harder really is the only way to go.

Viewing speeches as a learning opportunity and a chance to improve your communication skills is a healthy way of viewing an otherwise stressful and frightening experience. This is the mindset all beginning speakers must use when taking their first strides toward becoming a more confident speaker. Consequently, after you speak more and more, and reflect more and more on how well you did and what you can do to improve (and process the feedback from others), eventually you will get to the point where speaking in public is both easy and rewarding.

Don't just take my word for it. In addition to asking my public speaking classes why speaking in public is so frightening, I also asked them what is the best way to overcome this fear. A sampling of the more consistent responses follows:

- "I think being comfortable in front of your audience is the most important thing for a speaker, and that comes with practice—practicing and constantly having to do it."
- "The best way to overcome your fear of speaking is to practice—you have to face your fears"
- "In order to improve, you have to give more speeches. Practice makes perfect!"

- "You can overcome this fear by talking more in front of groups and making presentations. Just practice."
- "The way I can overcome my fear of public speaking is to do it more."

The only way to improve your public speaking abilities is to practice speaking in public. Be positive and open minded about the experience and focus on what you did well and what you can do to improve. In time, you will develop your own speaking style, at which others will marvel.

However, as stated earlier, if you avoid practicing or just go through the motions, you will hardly improve your public speaking abilities. Each speaking experience will be mediocre at best, and you will not achieve maximum speaking success. The costs of not controlling your fear of public speaking can harm your personal and professional advancement in life.

THE COSTS OF NOT CONTROLLING YOUR PUBLIC SPEAKING FEAR

If you choose to be a victim of public speaking and never confront your fears, you are really killing any chances of being effective in front of an audience. People will tune you out, focus more on your nervous gestures, not believe in what you are saying, and may be offended because they feel you are wasting their time. Obviously, if you take the time to prepare a speech, you at least want to avoid a poor speaking performance because if you don't, you are wasting *your* time. Think about what you may miss out on in life if your audience is not interested in what you have to say.

I asked my students what they felt were the costs associated with allowing fear to control a speaking performance. Some of their insights are better than anything I could have said:

- "People don't pay attention to you and they won't take you seriously."
- "If you give a poor public speech, due to fear, people may feel as though you do not really care about your work and that you are unprepared. People may not respect you as much. It gives others an idea of how you work in groups, and they may not want to work with you."
- "If a person is a poor speaker, they might not get a job or interview because they are not able to speak well. This could be avoided by practicing speaking."
- "A poor speech can keep one from getting a better job, or advance in life, for that matter. People tend not to listen to poor speakers."
- "If you let your fear harm your speech, the audience may realize you are unprepared and they will not learn anything from listening to you speak."

You owe it to yourself to practice speaking in public and focusing on overcoming any fears you may have about public speaking. If you avoid practicing public speaking, you will only be improving the chances of you not improving your speaking voice. How costly will that be to you and your professional and personal goals?

"What we have to learn to do, we learn by doing."

Aristotle

CHAPTER REFLECTION

1. If you fear public speaking, even slightly, take a few moments to reflect on why you may be fearful of speaking in public. Being able to understand your public speaking fears is the first step toward overcoming them.

2. If you are fearful of speaking in public, brainstorm strategies on how you think you may be able to overcome your fear.

3. What are the advantages of improving your public speaking abilities?

4. Select someone whom you feel is a polished public speaker and ask them how they manage their fear of speaking in public. Reflect on their advice below.

Chapter 3

Types Of Speaking Occasions And How To Prepare For Them

"Chance favors only the mind that is prepared."
Louis Pasteur

Immutable Truth #3:

If you speak unprepared or *wing it*, 998 times out of 1000 your performance will be awful. One time you may get lucky and another time you may "fool" your audience enough and deliver a decent speech.

Imagine you have a very important job interview tomorrow at 2:00 pm, with XYZ Company in their main office building downtown. You have already practiced interviewing, updated your resume, selected your interview clothes, and identified samples of your work you want to bring in order to better "sell" your skills. You are feeling pretty confident right now and then it hits you: you have no idea where XYZ Company is located downtown. Although you have been downtown before and remember passing by XYZ Company, you really cannot remember exactly where it is.

What do you do? You could either get in your car tomorrow and start driving downtown, hoping to find it. Or, you could look up the company's address in the phonebook, see exactly how to get there (what roads to take), and possibly do a practice drive-by today. On your practice run you find the roads to be under construction and once you arrive at XYZ Company's office building you realize the nearest parking garage is a block away. The construction delays and walk from the parking garage could add another twenty minutes to your travel time tomorrow. If you chose to plan ahead like this then you increase the chances of having a smooth commute to your interview.

The same principles of planning ahead holds true for speaking in public: in order to speak well you must prepare beforehand. Only through preparation can you attempt to speak well, and that will be the focus of this chapter: how to plan for informative and demonstration speeches.

EXIGENCE

The best way to determine how to prepare for a speech is to ask yourself the following questions:

- what/who prompted the speech? (why am I speaking?)

- from this "prompting" what might be the expectations for this speech? (what should I speak about and how should I go about it? How long am I expected to speak?)

If you can determine the answers to these questions you will have a smoother time preparing for your speech. As in the interview example, if you know your destination and how to best get there, the chances of arriving at your destination are much greater.

What brings about the speech, or prompts it, is called the *exigence*. The word exigence (from exigency) has been around since the 1500's and can best be defined as a *state of affairs that makes urgent demands.* Communication scholar Lloyd Bitzer set forth his ideas on rhetorical exigence in 1968 in *Philosophy and Rhetoric*, and these notions have evolved into a practical way to evaluate a speech. The notion essentially states that whatever and whoever calls a speech into being shall hold the criteria for speech success as well.

For example, when Pearl Harbor was bombed on December 7, 1941 by the Japanese Navy and Air Force, the United States was caught off-guard and frightened. The U.S., up until that point, was trying to avoid becoming a part of the war. The sneak attack at dawn caught the armed forces by surprise and severely damaged the U.S. military resources and personnel. President Franklin Delano Roosevelt, as a result of the tragedy, spoke to the American public to calm a shocked nation, express grief for the loss of life, and detail how the U.S. tried to remain uninvolved in the war. Also, for both the national and international audience, Roosevelt declared that he would authorize the U.S. to defend itself and then become involved in the war. The sneak attack was the exigence, or what prompted his speech. How his speech was to be evaluated was based on this *and* the other aspects of the speaking situation: audience fears, international audience, and military involvement and response.

Roosevelt delivered a powerful speech, with passion and conviction; you knew, as a listener, that he meant business. Americans *needed* that speech to quell fears and call for patriotism for their country. Further, if Roosevelt came out unprepared, monotone, uncaring, and unwilling to defend his country, how well do you think his speech would have been received by the American people? What about the international audience?

In speech class, an exigence could be your instructor assigning a speech, and discussing what elements of the speech process to focus on. For example, "Next Friday, be prepared to deliver a 6-8 minute informative speech, using the organizational pattern we discussed in class. Also, avoid saying 'um,' maintain appropriate eye contact, and incorporate an effective rate—not too fast and not too choppy and slow."

DETERMINING YOUR SPEECH PURPOSE

After you understand the exigence surrounding your speech, the next step would be to narrow the focus of your speech topic. Having said this, you can focus on narrowing your speech by determining 1) the speech's general purpose, 2) the speech's specific purpose, and 3) the speech's purpose statement.

General Purpose

Of all of the speeches that we could give, there are only three types, or general purposes, of speeches:

- Speeches to inform (enhance audience's knowledge about a specific topic)
- Speeches to persuade (to alter audience's belief and/or behavior)
- Speeches to entertain (lighthearted, amusing speeches—toasts and roasts, for example)

The focus of this book is to prepare you for the first type of general purpose: speeches to inform, which we will explore later in the chapter. After you develop your skills in the informative arena, you can then move on to the other two types, persuading and entertaining.

If you know what your exigence is, yet have a hard time narrowing your topic, determine what your general purpose is. Sometimes it will be given to you ("You have an informative speech due next Friday."), other times it may not be so clear. If you have a hard time trying to determine what your general purpose is, determine what it is you are being asked to do or what prompted the speech (i.e. what is the exigence?).

Specific Purpose

Your specific purpose narrows the focus of your speech by stating exactly your speech intentions in one sentence. Think of it like this: if you have one goal to achieve in your speech, then this goal would be your specific purpose. I think a few examples would be helpful in understanding what exactly a specific purpose is.

Imagine that your speech instructor has asked you to deliver an informative speech on any topic next week. You then would have to select a topic (you elect to do a speech on the history of Ohio) and narrow it down into a general and specific purpose:

General Purpose: To inform
Specific Purpose: To inform my audience about the history of Ohio

Here are some other examples of effective specific purposes:
Specific Purpose: To inform my audience about heart disease
Specific Purpose: To explain how zoos are funded
Specific Purpose: To explain how my communication style would be an asset for the professional field I want to enter

Remember, your specific purpose should be one sentence, as the above examples indicate. Your specific purpose is the road map that drives your speech preparation and focus.

Purpose Statement

Your speech's purpose statement, generally, is the same as your specific purpose, yet with a slight addition to the beginning of the sentence. You will, in the introduction of your speech, tell the audience what your speech is about, and this is known as the purpose statement. You would come out and directly say it in the introduction of your speech: "**Today, I am here** to inform you about heart disease." Or, "**Tonight, I will** explain how zoos are funded."

Knowing the general purpose, specific purpose, and purpose statement is necessary to structure your speech for effectiveness. Knowing these elements will allow you to focus specifically on your speech development and not drift in your preparation or focus. Also, coming out in the introduction and saying what your speech is about is necessary as it piques your audience's interest and develops goodwill and trust (they know you are not trying to hide anything from them).

INFORMATIVE SPEECHES EXPLAINED

It is necessary to focus now on what exactly an informative speech is, and how to prepare for them. Informative speeches are *about something* or address *how to do something* (demonstration speeches). Essentially, informative speeches:

- Enhance the audience's knowledge about a given topic
- Provide relevant information and details which advance audience's knowledge about a particular subject
- Include demonstration type speeches (how to change a tire, how to write a resume…)
- Include supporting material to strengthen claims (statistics, quotes, and testimony; also, visual aids)

Informative speeches are not meant to amuse an audience or be a joke, and are not intended to alter an audience's behaviors or attitudes. Informative speeches just focus on *increasing audience knowledge about a particular subject.*

So, by increasing an audience's knowledge about a subject, we could essentially have two types of informative speeches: 1) the informative speech in the most strict sense, and 2) demonstration speeches.

Informative Speech In The Most Strict Sense

Again, informative speeches are *about* something—about people, places, things, events (whether they happened or were alleged to have happened), and concepts. Further, the speech could inform the audience about the background of a famous person, history of the United States, different types of fishing rods, cause of the stock market crash in 1929, explanation of a certain management philosophy, and so on. Can you think of others?

Main Body Development

After narrowing down your topic, it would be advisable to strategically organize your speech (i.e. how you want the speech to flow) through a main body focus. *Main body points* advance and support your purpose statement, between the introduction and conclusion. For example, your specific purpose is to inform the audience about high blood pressure, two possible main body points could be:

- Main body point #1: the causes of high blood pressure
- Main body point #2: the effects of high blood pressure
- Note: depending on the exigence (time limits, audience needs,...), you may need three or more main body points

The above example illustrates a **cause and effect** type of main body point development. That is, you organized the speech around the cause of something and then you discussed the effects of the cause. Other types of main body point development (abbreviated MBP):

- Spatial—organize your speech via direction or physical layout of topic. An informative speech about the different regions of the U.S. (MBP #1: North; MBP #2: South; MBP #3: East; and MBP #4: West) is an example of a spatial pattern

- Chronological—organize your speech in historical order of events, from beginning to end. An informative speech about the different U.S. wars (MBP #1: Revolutionary War; MBP #2: Civil War; MBP #3: World War I; and MBP #4: World War II is an example of a chronological pattern)
- Topical—organize your speech via subtopics of a larger topic; not separate topics, but subtopics of a whole. An informative speech about the U.S. (MBP #1: U.S. goods/services produced; MBP #2: important people in U.S. history; and MBP #3: important U.S. inventions)

Using examples, statistics, testimony, and quotes that support your main points lends credence to your statements, and further assists in enhancing the audience's knowledge of the topic (more information on supporting material will be covered in a later chapter).

Demonstration Speeches

Demonstration speeches increase audience knowledge about *how to do something,* usually a *process*. A process arranges speaking topics in sequential order, with a specific end or goal in mind. A speaker may find it easier to determine the final outcome (or the ending point) of the process and then determine the steps needed to reach the goal.

General Purpose: To inform

Specific Purpose: To inform my audience how to trim their waistlines

Purpose Statement: "I am here today to inform you how you can trim your waistline."

Main Body Point #1: Diet

Main Body Point #2: Stomach exercises (crunches, leg raises, and sit-ups, with demonstration)

Main Body Point #3: Cardiovascular exercises (such as running)

As you can see, a demonstration speech may call you to actually demonstrate what you are talking about, as the above example illustrates. Actually showing (and explaining at the same time) your audience the proper techniques for the stomach exercises is more helpful than just explaining them. The extent to which you demonstrate the process should be influenced by the exigence (with a focus on audience needs). Other examples of demonstration speeches: how to calculate your mortgage payments; how to lower your blood pressure; how to effectively carry out a job search; how to negotiate a raise, and so on.

As you can see, the possible list of demonstration topics could go on for quite a while and can include everyday processes. However, what is everyday and easy to you may not be easy for your audience, which is why demonstration speeches are important. Demonstration speeches help the audience understand complex processes that yield specific results.

Focusing on the exigence, the purposes, intricacies of informative speeches, and main body point order go a long way toward public speaking success. If you allow these notions to guide your preparations you will find that your speech will be more focused, and therefore strategically effective. Being strategically effective is much better for you and your audience than just winging it.

"The desire to have things done quickly prevents their being done thoroughly."

Confucius

CHAPTER REFLECTION

1. Define exigence in your own words. Further, reflect on the events of September 11, 2001 and the exigence for President George W. Bush's speech later in the day. Fully describe the exigence that faced President Bush and analyze how effective/ineffective he was (his speech is at the end of this chapter).

2. Use the four different types of main body point order (cause and effect, spatial, chronological, and topical) to develop a specific purpose and three main points for an informative speech on your field of study or careers in your field.

3. Follow up on Lloyd Bitzer's analysis of exigence and the rhetorical situation. Start by reading his article "The Rhetorical Situation" in *Philosophy and Rhetoric*, 1, (1968): 1-14. Detail how his insights should impact the beginning speaker.

George W. Bush, President of the United States

September 11, 2001

Delivered in the White House to the nation

Good evening. Today, our fellow citizens, our way of life, our very freedom came under attack in a series of deliberate and deadly terrorist acts. The victims were in airplanes, or in their offices; secretaries, businessmen and women, military and federal workers; moms and dads, friends and neighbors. Thousands of lives were suddenly ended by evil, despicable acts of terror. The pictures of airplanes flying into buildings, fires burning, huge structures collapsing, have filled us with disbelief, terrible sadness, and a quiet, unyielding anger. These acts of mass murder were intended to frighten our nation into chaos and retreat. But they have failed; our country is strong.

A great people has been moved to defend a great nation. Terrorist attacks can shake the foundations of our biggest buildings, but they cannot touch the foundation of America. These acts shattered steel, but they cannot dent the steel of American resolve. America was targeted for attack because we're the brightest beacon for freedom and opportunity in the world. And no one will keep that light from shining.

Today, our nation saw evil, the very worst of human nature. And we responded with the best of America—with the daring of our rescue workers, with the caring for strangers and neighbors who came to give blood and help in any way they could.

Immediately following the first attack, I implemented our government's emergency response plans. Our military is powerful, and it's prepared. Our emergency teams are working in New York City and Washington, D.C. to help with local rescue efforts.

Our first priority is to get help to those who have been injured, and to take every precaution to protect our citizens at home and around the world from further attacks.

The functions of our government continue without interruption. Federal agencies in Washington which had to be evacuated today are reopening for essential personnel tonight, and will be open for business tomorrow. Our financial institutions remain strong, and the American economy will be open for business, as well.

The search is underway for those who are behind these evil acts. I've directed the full resources of our intelligence and law enforcement communities to find those responsible and to bring them to justice. We will make no distinction between the terrorists who committed these acts and those who harbor them.

I appreciate so very much the members of Congress who have joined me in strongly condemning these attacks. And on behalf of the American people, I thank the many world leaders who have called to offer their condolences and assistance.

America and our friends and allies join with all those who want peace and security in the world, and we stand together to win the war against terrorism. Tonight, I ask for your prayers for all those who grieve, for the children whose worlds have been shattered, for all whose sense of safety and security has been threatened. And I pray they will be comforted by a power greater than any of us, spoken through the ages in Psalm 23: "Even though I walk through the valley of the shadow of death, I fear no evil, for You are with me."

This is a day when all Americans from every walk of life unite in our resolve for justice and peace. America has stood down enemies before, and we will do so this time. None of us will ever forget this day. Yet, we go forward to defend freedom and all that is good and just in our world. Thank you. Good night, and God bless America.

Chapter 4

Introductions, Internal Summaries, Transition Statements, and Conclusions

"The beginning is the most important part of the work."

Plato

Immutable Truth #4:

A speech that rambles and seems unorganized will lose the audience. Not only will they "tune you out," but they will view you as unprepared and as a waste of their time.

After you come to understand what your exigence is and what your speech purposes are, and what your main body points will be, it is time to start drafting the outline of your speech. However, you cannot draft an outline of your speech without an introduction, internal summaries and transition statements, and a conclusion. This chapter will focus on these necessary elements as they are needed for your speech to flow well and sound polished to your audience.

WHY ORGANIZATION?

First, it is imperative for you to understand why organization is so important for speakers of all levels:

- An organized speech maintains the audience's interest more as it is easier for your audience to follow and pay attention to your main body points
- Because audiences have a greater tendency to pay attention to an organized speech, you have a greater chance of advancing your message. The audience will better absorb the material and have a greater understanding of your specific purpose
- An organized speech can enhance your credibility because as the audience sees it, anything a speaker can do to make a speech easier to follow and understand is much appreciated. This appreciation, in turn, helps your credibility
- An organized speech (if you have rehearsed and practiced your speech) can help you with your delivery. The more you know your speech and how it will flow, the more effective your delivery can be. Why? You can reduce vocal clutter such as "um" or "uh" (these are typically uttered when a speaker doesn't know what they will say

next) and your eye contact may be improved (you may not have to rely on your notes as much)

- Finally, organization can increase confidence because if you know what you are talking about and how your speech will flow, you will automatically believe in yourself and your specific purpose. Your confident energy will be noticed by the audience and they will appreciate your energy

Not only will you experience the above benefits associated with an organized speech, but you will also avoid the embarrassment of fumbling over your words, losing your place in your note cards, reading straight from your note cards, and speaking in a monotone (dry and without emotion) voice. The first step toward organization is developing an introduction, and the next section will explore tips on how to develop introductions effectively.

INTRODUCTIONS

Not surprisingly, introductions are at the beginning of the speech and are used to engage the audience right away. A poorly developed introduction will leave your audience wondering what your speech is about and why they should listen to you. A quality introduction should grasp the audience's attention by relating the topic to them, establish your credibility, discuss your purpose statement, preview your main body points, and provide a smooth transition to the main body of your speech. Generally, if an audience is to listen to the main body of your speech you need to get their attention quickly via an effective introduction.

Further, a quality introduction is critical for two reasons. First, by discussing your specific purpose and previewing your main points, you can give the audience an idea of what the speech is about. Therefore, a quality introduction makes it easier for the audience to pay attention. Secondly, it creates interest in the speech in the audience's mind.

So, how specifically, do speakers organize an effective introduction? The following are the six elements needed in effective introductions:

A. Attention Getter
B. Relevance To Audience
C. Establishment Of Credibility (also known as Ethos)
D. Purpose Statement
E. Preview Of Main Body Points
F. Transition To Main Body

Let's break these elements down individually to get a better idea of what exactly they entail.

A. Attention Getter: startling statement, best used with statistics or a quote; also use personal story or story of significant meaning from someone else; ask rhetorical questions with explanations; relevant song lyrics or lines of poetry. Can you think of other examples?

B. **Relevance To Audience**: link topic (specific purpose) to the interests/needs/desires/fears of the audience—helps to reinforce your attention getter. Could use statistics here as well.

C. **Establishment Of Credibility (Ethos)**: highlight why you think you are qualified to speak on the topic. Expand on how the topic impacted your life and what you did because of it. Also, could discuss how you have spent many hours researching topic due to your interest or for speech preparation.

D. **Purpose Statement**: specifically state why you are there to speak to the audience: *today, I am here to inform (or persuade) you about the benefits of aerobic exercise...*

E. **Preview Of Main Body Points**: continuation of purpose statement, only highlighting the specifics of the speech (the main body points). ***First****, I will look at how aerobic exercise is good for the circulation of blood.* **Second (or next)**, *I will examine how your blood pressure and cholesterol will be positively effected.* ***Finally****, I will discuss how aerobic exercise is good for managing stress.*

F. **Transition To Main Body**: make a smooth transition to the first main body point. *To begin, let's examine how aerobic exercise is good for the circulation of blood.*

These elements may seem to be a lot of information to cover, yet that is why these elements are so relevant. Without them, your audience will wonder what your speech is about, why they should listen to you, and what is in it for them. Do you want that? After you become familiar with these elements, you can pick and choose which elements to use in your introduction, depending on the exigence. Until then, commit to developing all of these elements in your early speeches.

To better understand how these elements lend themselves to an effective introduction, reflect on the following speech example:

General Purpose: To inform
Specific Purpose: To inform my audience on how to lose weight
Purpose Statement: "Today I am here to inform you about the steps you should take in order to lose weight."
Main Body Point #1: See a physician
Main Body Point #2: Incorporate a healthy diet into your lifestyle
Main Body Point #3: Start a physical exercise program

(**Attention Getter**) I recently visited my doctor, Dr. Smith, for a routine health exam. While I was there he told me that one out of every five people in the United States is considered overweight. Dr. Smith also said that one out of every three Americans will experience health problems due to being overweight. These health problems include high blood pressure, hypertension, shortness of breath during physical activity, and the possibility of suffering a fatal heart attack. (**Relevance To Audience**) Based on Dr. Smith's statistics, approximately eight people in this class, either are or will become, overweight. Furthermore, and even more startling, approximately three people in this classroom may eventually experience high blood pressure or even a fatal heart attack. (**Establishment Of Credibility/Ethos**) My father suffered a heart attack from being overweight, and I took it upon myself to research strategies that might prevent heart attacks. I have devoted many hours to reading health journals and books on the topic of being overweight, knowing that this knowledge may help prevent me from experiencing the pain my father has. (**Purpose Statement**) I will share this knowledge with you as today I am here to inform you on the steps you should take in order to lose weight. (**Preview Of Main Body Points**) First, I will discuss the importance of seeing a physician before starting any diet and exercise program. Second, I will explore the importance of incorporating a healthy diet into your lifestyle. Finally, I will touch on the importance of starting a physical exercise program. (**Transition To Body**) Now then, let's look at our first point: the importance of seeing a physician before starting a diet and exercise program.

Once you read through the example, you can notice how well the information flows together and how the information pertains to the audience. Further, there is no question as to why the speaker is qualified to speak on the topic and the direction (i.e. main body points) of the speech.

INTERNAL SUMMARIES AND TRANSITION STATEMENTS

In addition to establishing an organized tone for your speech in the introduction, organization is needed within the body of the speech, in between main body points. This organization comes in the form of *internal summaries* (IS) and *transition statements* (TS). As stated IS and TS's are used in between main body points and help the speaker move from one main point to the next. The internal summary will remind the listener of the main body point they just heard and the transition statement will preview the next main body point. Referring back to our *how to lose weight* speech, notice the internal summaries and transition statements between the main body points (note: A and B under the main body points are called *sub-points*, and are how the main body points will be developed by the speaker):

Main Body Point #1: See a physician

A. Obtain health exam and target health areas for improvement
B. Obtain recommended diet and exercise program

Internal Summary: Not only should you see a physician

Transition Statement: But you should also incorporate a healthy diet into your lifestyle

Main Body Point #2: Incorporate a healthy diet into your lifestyle

A. Understand and respect your daily caloric intake
B. Balance sugars, fats, proteins, and carbohydrates according to your health needs

Internal Summary: In addition to maintaining a healthy diet
Transition Statement: You should also start a physical exercise program

Main Body Point #3: Start a physical exercise program

A. Balance aerobic and weight training exercise according to your health needs
B. Try not to do too much too fast—stay focused and stick to the program

Internal Summary: Now that we have explored all of these tips
Transition Statement: Let's take a moment and recap

Conclusion (to be developed in the next section)

Integrating IS and TS's into your speech will enable you to look polished and well prepared as a speaker and keep your audience focused on your points. Also, in longer speeches (fifteen minutes and up), IS and TS's serve to break up the speech into sections, and encourages the audience to follow along (and catch up with you, if they have missed some of your information).

CONCLUSIONS

Just as the introduction sets the tone and creates interest for the speech, the conclusion recaps the essence of the speech via the following three elements:

A. Review Purpose Statement
B. Review Main Body Points
C. Clincher (Tie To Attention Getter)

Let's break these elements down individually to get a better idea of what exactly they entail.

A. **Review Purpose Statement**: repeat purpose statement. *Today I have informed you about the benefits of aerobic exercise;*
B. **Review Main Body Points**: recap the main points. *First, I looked at...Second, I examined...And finally, I explained...*
C. **Clincher (Tie To Attention Getter)**: end with emphasis. Link back to the opening attention getter that you developed in the introduction. Brings the speech full circle and shows how polished and well-prepared you were.

Based on the introduction and main points of the *how to lose weight* speech, a possible conclusion could be the following:

(**Review Purpose Statement**) Today I have informed you on the steps you should take in order to lose weight. (**Review Main Body Points**) First, I discussed the importance of seeing a physician before starting a diet and exercise program. Second, I shared with you the need for incorporating a healthy diet into your lifestyle. Third, and finally, I discussed the importance of starting a physical exercise program. (**Clincher/Tie To Attention Getter**) I hope that you have learned more about losing weight and will pay attention to the lifestyle you lead. I do not want to read in the paper, thirty years from now, about one of you dying from a heart attack. I do not want to wonder which of you will make up the other two people who may suffer a heart attack. Thank you.

(Note: A complete outline of the *how to lose weight* speech can be viewed at the end of the chapter)

The more you practice strategically developing this type of conclusion, the easier and more effective it will become. Consequently, you will be able to make the ending of your speech flow very smoothly, which will leave your audience impressed and wanting more. Further, your audience will come to know that you really thought out your speech, from beginning to end, and will be very appreciative of your efforts (which may result in the audience assigning more credibility to you).

Developing introductions, IS and TS's, and conclusions will carry your message far in the eyes of your audience, as you make it easy on them to follow your speech. If the audience finds it easier to follow your speech, they will more likely pay attention to your message, and not view your speech as a waste of time.

"A good beginning makes a good ending."

English Proverb

CHAPTER REFLECTION

1. As an audience member, why do you feel it is important for a speaker to organize his/her speech with an introduction, internal summaries and transition statements, and a conclusion?

2. The following are the first two main body points of an informative speech on the importance of investing money. Write an internal summary and transition statement in the space provided.

   Main Body Point #1: Determine your current financial situation

   A. Assess your expenses and income
   B. Assess your monthly budget

   Internal Summary:

   Transition Statement:

Main Body Point #2: Determine your future financial goals

A. Estimate expenses/income for relevant points in the future (i.e. retirement)

B. Consult a relevant Financial Planner

3. This chapter, you read about the word *ethos*. Research the origin and history of *ethos*, along with *pathos* and *logos*, while focusing on their implications for public speakers.

Outline For *How To Lose Weight* Speech

It is recommended beginning speakers prepare for their speeches using the following organizational pattern

General Purpose: To inform
Specific Purpose: To inform my audience on how to lose weight
Purpose Statement: "Today I am here to inform you about the steps you should take in order to lose weight."
Main Body Point #1: See a physician
Main Body Point #2: Incorporate a healthy diet into your lifestyle
Main Body Point #3: Start a physical exercise program

(**Attention Getter**) I recently visited my doctor, Dr. Smith, for a routine health exam. While I was there he told me that one out of every five people in the United States is considered overweight. Dr. Smith also said that one out of every three Americans will experience health problems due to being overweight. These health problems include high blood pressure, hypertension, shortness of breath during physical activity, and the possibility of suffering a fatal heart attack. (**Relevance To Audience**) Based on Dr. Smith's statistics, approximately eight people in this class, either are or will become, overweight. Furthermore, and even more startling, approximately three people in this classroom may eventually experience high blood pressure or even a fatal heart attack. (**Establishment Of Credibility/Ethos**) My father suffered a heart attack from being overweight, and I took it upon myself to research strategies that might prevent heart attacks. I have devoted many hours to reading health journals and books on the topic of being overweight, knowing that this knowledge may help prevent me from experiencing the pain my father has. (**Purpose Statement**) I will share this knowledge with you as today I am here to inform you on the steps you should take in order to lose weight. (**Preview Of Main Body Points**) First, I will discuss the importance of seeing a physician before starting any diet and exercise program. Second, I will explore the importance of incorporating a healthy diet into your lifestyle. Finally, I will touch on the importance of starting a physical exercise program. (**Transition To Body**) Now then, let's look at our first point: the importance of seeing a physician before starting a diet and exercise program.

Main Body Point #1: See a physician

A. Obtain health exam and target health areas for improvement
B. Obtain recommended diet and exercise program

Internal Summary: Not only should you see a physician

Transition Statement: But you should also incorporate a healthy diet into your lifestyle

Main Body Point #2: Incorporate a healthy diet into your lifestyle

A. Understand and respect your daily caloric intake
B. Balance sugars, fats, proteins, and carbohydrates according to your health needs

Internal Summary: In addition to maintaining a healthy diet

Transition Statement: You should also start a physical exercise program

Main Body Point #3: Start a physical exercise program

A. Balance aerobic and weight training exercise according to your health needs
B. Try not to do too much too fast and stick to the program

Internal Summary: Now that we have explored all of these tips

Transition Statement: Let's take a moment and recap

(**Review Purpose Statement**) Today I have informed you on the steps you should take in order to lose weight. (**Review Main Body Points**) First, I discussed the importance of seeing a physician before starting a diet and exercise program. Second, I shared with you the need for incorporating a healthy diet into your lifestyle. Third, and finally, I discussed the importance of starting a physical exercise program. (**Clincher/Tie To Attention Getter**) I hope that you have learned more about losing weight and will pay attention to the lifestyle you lead. I do not want to read in the paper, thirty years from now, about one of you dying from a heart attack. I do not want to wonder which of you will make up the other two people who may suffer a heart attack. Thank you.

Chapter 5

Audience Analysis And Supporting Material

"Everyone believes that what suits him is the right thing to do."

Goethe

Immutable Truth #5:
If your audience does not "connect" with your speech (i.e. they find it irrelevant), you will find it almost impossible to achieve your purpose statement.

One of the crucial elements of the exigence, that is, what prompted the speech, is the audience of the speech. The audience will influence much of how you organize your speech, what you include in (and leave out of) your speech, and your time constraints. Further, if the audience is not interested in your speech, the effectiveness of your speech suffers. Why? No matter how successful you thought your speech was, your opinion is only a fraction of measuring your speech's success. **The audience is the primary measuring stick in determining your speech's level of success.** If, as a result of listening to your speech, the audience becomes bored, offended, distracted, or doubts your credibility, then the likelihood of the audience accepting your speech's message will be minimal at best.

Generally, as a public speaker, you want your audience to do any number of things with the information contained in your speech:

- Accept your message
- Evaluate your message and draw conclusions
- Appreciate the significance of your message
- Take action after listening to your speech (in persuasion speeches)
- Alter their beliefs and choose your stance on a message (persuasion and debate speeches)

We do not speak in public for our health, we speak so the audience can understand and be influenced by our purpose statement. This chapter will focus on understanding your audience and how to influence them by using appropriate supporting material.

AUDIENCE ANALYSIS

First rule of audience analysis: whomever you speak to, tailor your message to them. Second rule of audience analysis: carefully analyze the characteristics of your audience prior to developing your speech and allow this characterization to help you tailor your message to them. The first rule should be easy to understand because without an audience we are not speaking publicly. The second rule is a little more complex, and this is where we will begin our discussion of audience analysis.

Grouping

Grouping (also called *segmenting* or *isolating*) is the practice of breaking your audience down into groups or segments based on similar characteristics, so as to better understand their needs and expectations (i.e. how to influence them). Grouping is beneficial because what may look like a random audience can be turned into an understood collection of individuals. You can group an audience in the following ways:

- Age
- Gender
- Familial background (heritage, national origin, etc.)
- Socio-economical status
- Professional level
- Knowledge of speech topic (a lot versus a little determines the direction of your speech)
- Political beliefs
- Religious beliefs

Can you think of other methods of grouping an audience? Now, just because you have identified the composition of an audience, this does not mean you are fully prepared to develop your speech. To better tailor your message to an audience, assess the grouping factors along with their impact needs, impact fears, and impact goals.

We all have an understanding what needs (see Abraham Maslow's hierarchy of needs) are—the need to eat, the need for good health, the need to achieve success, and the need to live a long successful life. Impact needs, however, are those needs that are more immediate to an audience; more the here and the now. If you were presenting your professional skills to a hiring manager in a job interview, his/her impact needs would be the need to hire the best candidate at the appropriate salary. Further, he/she would need to bring on board a candidate who can fit well within the organization (so other team members could work well with the candidate). Therefore, your presentation should be tailored to satisfy those impact needs.

Impact fears are the immediate fears of an audience. The hiring manager's immediate fear would be that he/she may not find a quality candidate and consequently, business operations may be interrupted. Also, the hiring manager may fear hiring someone who turns out to be a "flop" because the hiring manager is measured by the quality of candidates who are hired. The fear of looking like a failure in front of the V.P. of Human Resources would be an immediate impact fear. An understanding of these impact fears could help the candidate strategically tailor the message of his/her presentation.

Impact goals are, as you probably guessed, immediate goals—objectives that have to be accomplished right now or in the very near future. An immediate goal of the hiring manager is to conduct the interview in its allotted time: one hour. The hiring manager has a hectic schedule after the interview and must achieve the one-hour objective. Another impact goal of the hiring manager would be to gather all of the information from you, the candidate, which addresses why you are qualified for the position. If the hiring manager is left to guess why you are qualified for the position, then chances are you will not move forward in the hiring process. Consequently, you have to respect the hiring manager's time by showing up on time (ten minutes early isn't bad either) and being prepared to succinctly discuss your qualifications in your allotted presentation time. If you fail to develop your ideas or ramble incoherently about yourself and exceed the time limit, how impressed will the hiring manager be with you? Understanding the impact goals will further assist you in tailoring your message to your audience.

Be Advised, Though...

While it is smart for a speaker to group an audience, it is advisable that a speaker remains flexible in his/her planning and delivering of the speech. This is due in large part because:

- There may be different groups within an audience (the audience of a skills presentation in a job interview may include the hiring manager, a peer, a stakeholder, and a subordinate)

- Inferring too much about a group may lead to a stereotyping of their characteristics, which may mean you fail to recognize other impact needs, fears, and goals
- Over-assuming the impact needs, fears, or goals of a group may result in the failure to tailor your message correctly (a class composed mostly of males may indeed be interested in learning about the history of nursing—they may want to choose it as a career path or may have friends and family in the nursing field)

Ignoring this advice may poorly influence your speech preparation, which may result in a poorly tailored message. Consequently, the audience may "tune you out" or worse still, become offended. An offended audience may become disruptive and outspoken during your speech, which may further damage your credibility. The end result would be that your speech preparation time would be wasted, your credibility would be damaged, and a speaking event you would soon like to forget.

Matching your message with the impact needs, fears, and goals of your audience will strengthen your credibility and keep your audience interested in your message. One other way to ensure credibility and pique the interest of the audience is to integrate supporting material into your speech.

SUPPORTING MATERIAL

Supporting material is used by the speaker to advance the speaker's claims and strengthen a speaker's argument. Supporting material includes statistics, examples, and testimony from credible sources. Integrating these elements in a speech lends credence to your ideas (because what you say is explained or supported by a source citation) and helps your audience better understand your message.

Statistics

Statistics is the integration of percentages and other numbers (fractions, etc) to quantify your claims. For example, you could claim in your speech, on weather patterns in Cincinnati, "approximately two-thirds of the days in August in Cincinnati reach 90 degrees." The effects of integrating statistics into that statement are more profound than saying "the majority of the days in August in Cincinnati are hot."

Examples

Examples add more depth to a statement by developing an idea such that a mental picture can be created in the minds of the audience. In the same speech on weather patterns in Cincinnati, you could say "I remember last August driving into downtown Cincinnati on what seemed to be the hottest day of the year. My car's air conditioning was not working, and even though the windows were down, it felt hotter outside than it did inside. It was then, with sweat streaming down my face, that I noticed a temperature reading stating it was 97 degrees."

The audience can actually picture the temperature reading flashing 97 degrees and they could probably picture a car with its' windows down, with the driver miserable in the car. Integrating a developed example sounds better and provides more clarity than saying, "sometimes I have noticed it being really hot in the summer in Cincinnati."

Testimony

Testimony, also known as source citations, quotes a credible person's or agency's thoughts or analysis of a particular subject. For example, you could quote a Certified Public Accountant (CPA) on tax tips if you are speaking on how to prepare for tax season. Relating back to the speech on weather patterns in Cincinnati, you could quote a local Cincinnati meteorologist (person) or the National Weather Service (agency): "According to the National Weather Service, approximately two-thirds of the days in August in Cincinnati reach 90 degrees." Now, your statement is supported by an "expert" and your audience knows that you performed adequate research on your topic, and may assign more credibility to your claims.

An important note here: integrating testimony should mean that you limit the amount of using your opinions for evidence. Unless you are an expert in a certain field (worked or studied a particular field for at least five years), you should focus on replacing opinions with statements supported by testimony whenever you can. Too many opinions diminish the quality of your message because your opinions may be flawed. Further, too many opinions leads the audience to wonder how accurate your speech's information is, and therefore could lose focus on your intended message. Also, be sure to round complex numbers off, so you can integrate your facts smoothly without confusing your audience. For example, instead of saying, "we used 2,987 sheets of paper last week" you could say, "we used nearly 3,000 sheets of paper last week."

Be Advised, Though...

What is a "credible expert" source for testimony? Assess the following issues to determine if your source of testimony is credible:

- The internet has a lot of research material, and some of the material may be high quality and other material may be less credible. Almost anybody can develop a website and put anything on it. Determine the credentials of the person or agency who placed the information on the internet (did you read in somebody's online diary that August in Cincinnati is a hot month? Or did you obtain it from the National Weather Service?)

- Some of the information you read may be outdated, so check and see how recent the information is. Maybe the information on the National Weather Service's website is ten years old. Perhaps another, more recent (still credible) person or agency should be used—perhaps a meteorology periodical
- It is always advisable to seek testimony from diverse sources, so you can balance your claims and strengthen your message. Using both the National Weather Service and a Cincinnati meteorologist (perhaps two meteorologists) would suffice for our weather in Cincinnati speech. Further, the audience is *really* appreciative of this (as a speech instructor I can see it in their faces when a speaker integrates a number of relevant, diverse source citations and supporting material into a speech)

(Note: Tips on integrating source citations and testimony in speeches will be provided at the end of the chapter)

Understanding your audience and integrating supporting material that will best pique the audience's interest, while strengthening your claims, will go a long way in ensuring an effective presentation. Further, your audience will pay more attention to your ideas and assign more credibility to you as a speaker, which in turn could be used by you to strategically influence them the way your purpose statement desires.

"A world of facts lies outside and beyond the world of words."

Thomas Huxley

CHAPTER REFLECTION

1. Research Abraham Maslow's hierarchy of needs (see *Motivation and personality*, 2nd edition, New York: Harper & Row, 1970). From your analysis of his research on needs, discus the implications for public speakers when developing a speech.

2. Determine an audience you may find yourself speaking in front of in the near future. Assess their impact needs, impact fears, and impact goals.

3. Brainstorm at least three credible and diverse resources that you could use to research and support your ideas on the following informative speech topics:
   a. Summer weather trends in your city
   b. Careers in your industry or major
   c. History of your school or place of employment

Tips For Integrating Source Citations Into Your Speech

Interviews: "In a personal interview with Andrew Muench, former Army Captain and Apache Helicopter Pilot conducted on April 12, 2003, he said, 'Flying helicopters is fun, but dangerous.'" **Include:** Date of interview, person you interviewed, and their qualifications.

Journals/Magazines: "According to the June 2001 edition of *Bears And Bulls*, Skip Van Sant, Financial Planner and Editorial Contributor, claims '401(k) plans are worth looking into for generation X-ers.'" **Include:** Date of publication, author and if possible credentials, and title of journal/magazine.

Newspapers: "According to Fred Mills in his column in the September 22, 2002 edition of the *Orlando Times*, 'Ninety percent of all job applicants do not have an effective resume in the beginning of their job search process.'" **Include:** Author, date of publication, and newspaper the article is from.

Books: "According to Jim Slouffman's 2003 book The Art & Science of Teaching: Creating a Home For Learning, 'you will sometimes find students blaming others for their poor performance.'" **Include:** Name of author, name of book, date of book.

Internet Sites: "According to meteorologist Richard Handley's personal website, **www.rhweather.com**, based on his 2002 study, 'August 2002 was the hottest month of the year in Cincinnati, Ohio.'" **Include:** Date of study or when site was updated, author of website, and credentials of author or agency.

Chapter 6

Visual Aids

"One picture is worth more than a thousand words."
Anonymous

Immutable Truth #6:
The worst kind of visual aid is a sloppy visual aid, which doesn't enhance the audience's knowledge of your topic. However, as sad is it may sound, this is predominantly the kind of visual aid beginning speakers use.

While there are many things that need to come together to make a speech effective, sometimes all it takes is one or two things that may render a speech ineffective. Specifically, if a speech is properly organized, incorporates supporting material, appropriate for the audience, and conforms to time limits, the speech could still be a flop. Why? For two reasons: 1) poor use of visual aids, and 2) poor delivery. Both, when executed poorly, can harm a speaker's credibility and suck the life out of any speech. This chapter will focus on visual aid fundamentals, benefits of using visual aids, types of visual aids, and criteria for visual aid success. The next chapter will focus on delivery.

BENEFITS OF USING VISUAL AIDS

You may be asking yourself "why should I incorporate visual aids in my speech?" This is a good question, so let's look at the benefits of using visual aids.

- Interest—visual aids can help maintain audience's interest, as the content of the visual may "breathe" fresh air into the speech. A properly timed visual aid, containing the right information, can pique the audience's interest, and may arouse curiosity
- Retention—visual aids can help the audience remember key facts within your speech. Because the audience's interest is piqued, they may be more inclined to actively process your information, rather than sitting there passively, allowing your points to "sail over their heads"
- Simplicity—visual aids can help break complex information down for your audience, helping them to understand your ideas rather than becoming confused by them. For example, if you were discussing how to calculate a simple interest formula, you may want to include the formula, along with an example on a visual aid (poster board, perhaps). Wouldn't you think it would be

easier for an audience to process this formula after they see it?

- Perception—how well you use and the extent to which you use visual aids in your speech will influence how the audience perceives you. If you put together a quality visual aid (we will talk about the elements of a quality visual aid later in the chapter) your audience will assign more credibility to you than if you hastily threw together an uninformative, sloppy visual aid at the last minute
- Pacing—visual aids can regulate the pace, or flow, of a speech. Integrating a visual aid at the right time (at the end of a main point or at the beginning of another) can help break up the monotony of your speech, and help refocus the audience onto what you are saying (too much speaker monotony = a daydreaming audience)

TYPES OF VISUAL AIDS

There are probably hundreds of visual aids, and including all of them is beyond the scope of this book. From computer presentations to skits, and everything in between, visual aids all come back to one thing: enhancing the audience's knowledge about your subject. However, an introduction into some of the more basic types of visual aids, while emphasizing advantages, is useful and shall encourage you, the reader, to ask yourself: which visual aid would help enhance my audience's knowledge about my subject?

Bar Graphs

Bar graphs are effective for showing comparisons between two or more items. By using vertical or horizontal graphs, the material you are presenting can be illustrated for the audience, which might help them "see" the importance of what you are speaking about (an example is provided at the end of this chapter).

Line Graphs

Line graphs are very similar to bar graphs in that two or more things can be compared over time. However, line graphs can also pin-point accurate data in specific points in time. Consequently, your audience can "see" how your subject changes at different points in time or in different situations (an example is provided at the end of this chapter).

Pie Graphs

Pie graphs show proportions (usually in percentages) between or among two or more things. As a result of breaking your subject into proportions or percentages, the audience can "see" differences amongst the proportions, and draw conclusions based on its findings (an example is provided at the end of this chapter).

Summation Charts

Summation charts are effective in helping the audience retain key data and information. If particular points in your speech are long or complex, a summation chart could be used to "summarize" the key information before moving on to the next point in your speech. Further, a summation chart could also be used at the end of a speech (prior to or during the conclusion), recapping major ideas and or crucial data in order for your audience to better grasp the information (an example is provided at the end of this chapter).

Photographs

Photographs are used in a variety of public speaking formats to help the audience better understand the speaker's message. From courtroom debates to driver's license identification when you are pulled over by the police, pictures really do provide valuable information for its viewers. For example, if you are giving a speech on the effects of smoking, showing a photograph of a nonsmoker's lung compared to a smoker's lung could provide powerful imagery for your audience on the dangers of smoking.

Models

Models normally are replications of an object you are speaking about, and are used to enhance the audience's knowledge about that object. Models can be the actual size of the object (if you are giving an informative speech on antique lamps you could bring one in as an example), smaller than the actual object (if you are giving an informative speech on Christopher Columbus' 1492 voyage you could bring in a model of the ship he traveled on: the Santa Maria), or a blown-up version of the actual object (if you are giving an informative speech on the composition of atoms you could bring in a model of its atomic structure).

CRITERIA FOR VISUAL AID EFFECTIVENESS

After witnessing over three thousand speeches, I have seen some very effective visual aids, and unfortunately, some ineffective visual aids. All of the effective visual aids meet the following four criteria for visual aid success:

1) Large enough to be seen—whatever it is you are using, a photograph or a chart, the content has to be large enough for everybody in the audience to see. If the audience cannot see it, why waste time displaying it?
2) Enhance the audience's knowledge about your subject—try to put yourself in the audience's position and ask yourself, "if I were listening to this speech what would help me better understand its' content?" I once saw someone use an empty beer can for their only visual aid in an informative speech on the dangers of drunk driving. How effective do you think that was in enhancing the audience's knowledge about the dangers of drunk driving?

3) Print (whether handwritten or typed on a computer) has to be clean and not sloppy. Further, avoid print that appears to be too crowded because it makes it hard for the audience to read. If they cannot read the print, why waste time displaying it?
4) If you obtain your visual's information from a source, include that source at either the bottom or top of the visual. For example: Source: National Weather Service 2000 Survey on Ocean Currents

A visual aid should be strategically designed to enhance your audience's knowledge in order to make it easier for them to grasp your points. Understanding the benefits of visual aids, the different types of visual aids, and the criteria for visual aid effectiveness will allow you to use visual aids to your strategic advantage. It is up to you now to strategically plan ahead for your visual aid's success.

"Plans are nothing. Planning is everything."

Dwight D. Eisenhower

CHAPTER REFLECTION

1. As an audience member, why do you feel visual aids are effective for a speaker to use in a speech?

2. How would you define what an ineffective visual aid is? Discuss this definition and analyze the effects of a speaker using an ineffective visual aid when presenting to you.

3. Think about a speech or presentation you may give in the near future and determine at least two visual aids you could use. Further, analyze the visual aids according to the four criteria for visual aid effectiveness discussed in the last part of the chapter.

Visual Aid Examples: Bar Graph, Line Graph, Pie Graph, and Summation Chart

Please note—these visual aids were drawn by hand to illustrate how clear and effective hand-drawn visual aids can be. While computer presentations offer crisp images, a carefully drawn visual aid by hand can do just as well at times (if you have the discipline to put forth the necessary time). Do these four visual aid examples meet the four criteria for visual aid effectiveness outlined in the chapter?

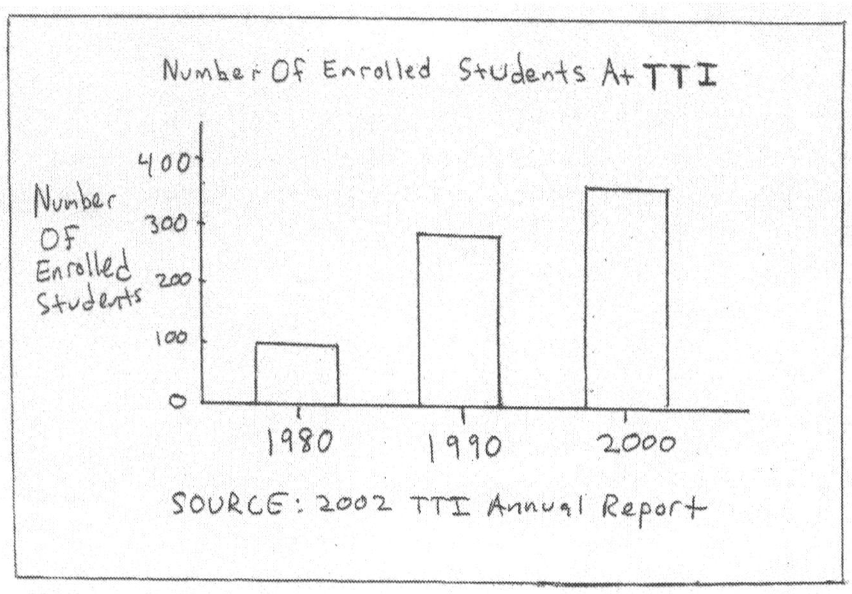

Bar Graph

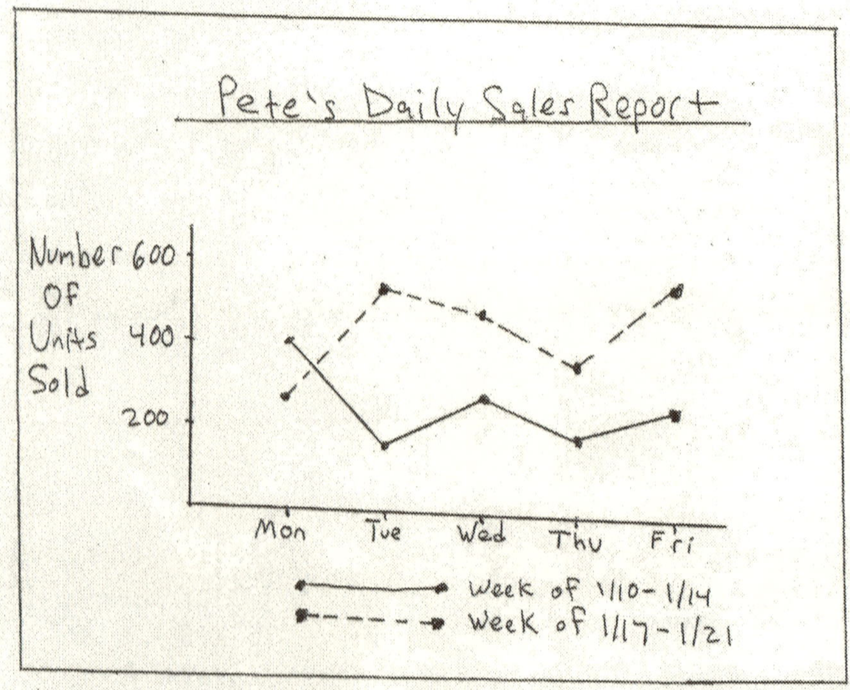
Pete's Daily Sales Report
Number Of Units Sold
600
400
200
Mon
Tue
Wed
Thu
Fri
Week of 1/10-1/14
Week of 1/17-1/21

Line Graph

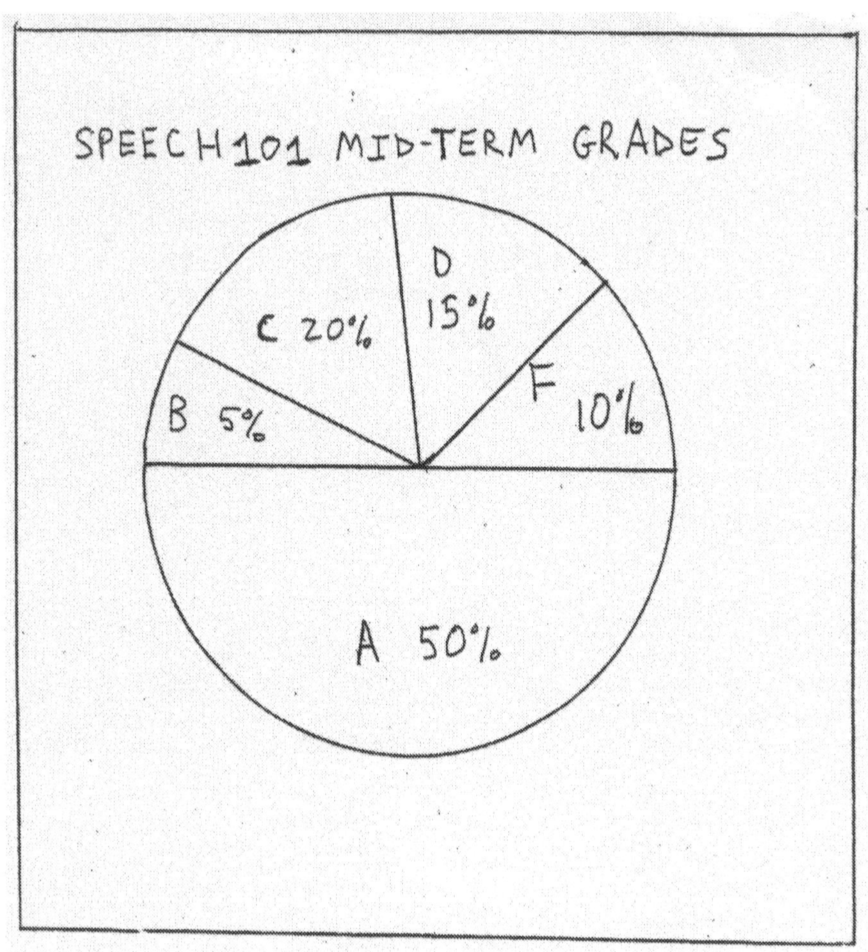

Pie Graph

Study Tips Reviewed

1. Attend class regularly and take notes on relevant material

2. Review notes after class and prior to the start of the next class

3. Begin studying for an exam four days in advance

Source: 7/10/03 Personal Interview with Walt Stockman, Academic Advisor

Summation Chart

Chapter 7

Delivery

"A man without a smiling face must not open a shop."

Chinese Proverb

Immutable Truth #7:

You can have the best speech in the world, organized to the smallest detail, but if you read straight from your notes in a monotone voice, within thirty seconds your audience would have lost the motivation to listen to you speak.

Your delivery, that is, your physical mannerisms, appearance, and voice, has a greater impact on your audience than you may think. As my public speaking classes start to focus on effective delivery, I ask them to think of someone who they feel is a good public speaker and share that individual's characteristics with the class. Students have mentioned everybody from Martin Luther King, Jr. to Ronald Reagan to Oprah Winfrey to British Prime Minister Tony Blair to instructors they have had in the past. When I ask the students why they chose those speakers, my students would invariably say, "because they kept my attention and spoke on the audience's level." The impact of good delivery equates to maintaining audience interest.

We have already explored audience needs—now we will explore how delivery is useful in keeping the audience interested in your speech. This chapter will explore the importance of delivery and strategies that you can use to make delivery work for you.

IMPORTANCE OF DELIVERY

I like to view the delivery aspect of public speaking in terms of *packaging*. Your physical mannerisms, appearance, and voice are all linked to how the audience pays attention to your speech—your delivery is a part of the package. I think a totally unrelated example would help you understand the notion of packaging.

Let's say you are in need of a 50-inch television for your den and are willing to spend $3,000 for a high-end model. You want a unit that will provide crisp images with awesome audio, DVD hook-up, and all of the other bells and whistles that could go along with a $3,000 television. You arrive at the television store and seek out assistance from a salesperson who enthusiastically shows you the television which matches your wish list. There is one problem though; the television is caked in mud and covered with dried paint. The monitor is cracked and the wires in the back look frayed. The salesperson, seeing the mortified expression on your face says, "Not to worry, it works fine. All you have to do is bang on the top of it and the picture and audio will come on. The picture may be a little fuzzy, but it will work."

Even though you can still watch the television and hear the content of the programs on it, you probably would not be interested in purchasing the model. The reason for your reluctance is how the whole television is packaged—it is in awful shape and does not meet your expectations for how a television should look. The same principle holds true for a public speaker—if your physical delivery is so bad that it detracts from your message, even though your audience can still hear your message, they will not buy into your speech. Remember I said in the beginning of this book that people will buy into you first before they buy into your ideas. You are the package they are trying to buy into. Make it easy on your audience to buy into your speech by incorporating effective delivery with your message.

PHYSICAL MANNERISMS

In terms of public speaking there are two broad types of physical mannerisms that public speakers tend to display. The first type is *distracting physical mannerisms*, in that because of their use in a speech, the audience focuses more on the physical mannerisms than the speaker's message. Obviously, distracting physical mannerisms should be avoided in a speech because one goal of a speech is to keep the audience's interest so they can concentrate on your message. Distracting mannerisms include:

- tapping your hands nervously on your podium
- playing with your watch in the middle of your speech
- excessively crossing your legs or shuffling your feet; doing so harms your posture too
- brushing your hair out of your eyes or behind your ear(s) excessively
- tapping your pen/pencil on the podium when speaking
- incorporating too many vocal fillers such as "um," "like," and "you know"
- smacking your lips when you speak
- "wringing" your hands
- monotone voice, generally resulting from reading directly from note cards

Essentially, any nervous physical (could be voice related, too) gesture that you integrate into your speech is distracting your audience away from your message.

Can you think of any other distracting physical mannerisms?

The second type of physical mannerisms can be called *strategic physical mannerisms*, as these mannerisms are used to reinforce your message and maintain audience interest. These mannerisms include:

- standing erect with your head up and shoulders back while looking at the audience
- keeping your legs still (so your body remains still and won't rock back and forth)

- using your hands only to strategically emphasize points; otherwise, keeping your hands still
- maintaining balanced eye contact with audience members
- avoiding other nervous gestures: lip smacking, vocal fillers,…

When in doubt, remain still except when emphasizing points, either with your hands and/or head. Before your speech, ask yourself: what can I do today in my delivery that will reinforce my ideas and not distract the audience? Be conscious of your movements and use them strategically to reinforce your message.

APPEARANCE

Your appearance—what you wear, how you comb your hair, your make-up, and so on, has to match the exigence and reinforce what you are saying. Further, your appearance should not be distracting or offensive, as you want to maintain the audience's interest. Generally, you should dress one level above what the audience will be wearing. If your audience is in jeans and t-shirts, you may want to wear a nice button-up shirt with khakis. If your audience is wearing khakis and nice button-up shirts, you could wear a suit. If your audience is in a suit, you should wear your best suit and tie, and in some occasions maybe a tuxedo.

Dressing appropriately will help you mentally prepare yourself as a public speaker. Some of my students believe that getting a little more dressed up for a speech helps in getting them focused on their delivery and concentration. It should also be noted that your audience will appreciate your effort to dress appropriately and may assign more credibility to you. After all, would you like to buy a television from a salesperson in a prison inmate outfit? Probably not. Your appearance is a part of your package whether you like it or not.

VOICE

I am sure you have heard the expression, "it is not what you say but how you say it." The way you use your voice in your speech can greatly influence your audience—you can make your speech very interesting or bore them with a monotonous speaking voice (one that is dull and boring). To make your speaking voice interesting, concentrate on the following characteristics: rate, pitch, and volume.

Rate

Your rate is the speed at which you speak. Some public speakers speak way too fast, harming the audience's ability to grasp information and key points. Other speakers have a slow…and…choppy…rate…where…they…never…seem…to pick… up any…steam. Work on a smooth and appropriate rate that matches your message and exigence. For example, it may be necessary to slow down your rate if you are trying to emphasize a powerful point, allowing your audience to soak in every last word. Use your best judgment and be strategic about it.

Pitch

Your pitch is the highness and lowness of your voice on a musical scale. It may be necessary to integrate a low pitch when emphasizing a sad story as a low pitch may be appropriate. On the other hand, when you are speaking on something that is very well received by the audience (good news), you could speak in a higher pitch to show excitement. Again, your pitch should be strategically linked to your message and exigence.

Volume

Volume, the loudness or softness of a speech, again must be strategic. Some speakers do not speak loud enough thus making it hard for their audience to hear them. If their audience has to strain to hear them it is possible that their audience may lose interest (let's be honest, some people are lazy and do not want put forth the effort to hear a speaker—they would rather daydream). Conversely, if a speaker is too loud the audience may become intimidated because they may feel the speaker is shouting or trying to demean them.

Balance your rate, pitch, and volume in order to avoid speaking in a monotonous voice, while strategically matching your message with the exigence.

One Other Thing...

It should be noted that a speaker has to have the right mindset to speak: confident, positive, and strategic. Even if you are nervous, try not to outwardly show it. Even if you were assigned a topic which you do not particularly like, do not let your distaste show. Giving these clues away makes it harder for your audience to buy into you. A good speaker, with the proper delivery and topic development can make a bland topic more interesting to the audience. Commit to thinking like this and discipline yourself in preparing strategic delivery. Remember, you are the person responsible for how the audience views your speech. Package yourself accordingly.

A polished speaker is mindful of his/her physical mannerisms, appearance, and voice because of how these characteristics can influence an audience. Strategic delivery that reinforces the message is necessary for maintaining audience interest and encouraging the audience to buy in. Maintaining a positive attitude toward delivery is necessary in the beginning stages because delivery is one of the tougher aspects for beginning speakers to command. In time, through practice and commitment, strategic delivery can be as easy as riding a bike.

"Let deeds match words."

Plautus

CHAPTER REFLECTION

1. Pick anybody who you feel is an effective public speaker and analyze their characteristics according to the following:
   a. Why do you feel he/she is effective at speaking in public?
   b. What are the characteristics they exhibit which make them effective?
   c. Discuss the speaker's effect on you (when you are listening to them, how do you feel?)

2. List some distracting physical mannerisms you have seen speakers do and discuss how those mannerisms impacted you as an audience member.

3. List out your distracting physical mannerisms and reflect on what you can do to control them. Also, reflect on your strategic physical mannerisms and determine why you are using them when speaking.

Chapter 8

Other Tips For The Beginning Speaker

"The spirit of the thing lives in the details."
Mies van der Rohe

Immutable Truth #8:
If you choose to be successful and prepare for success, you will be successful.

In order to assist you in your development toward becoming a confident and effective public speaker, I feel it would be appropriate to give you some final speech preparation tips. Some of these tips were emphasized in the book quite well and other tips were more peripheral, yet still necessary. These tips are what every beginning speaker should know and respect in order to become the public speaker they want to be.

What To Do Before The Speech

- Approach public speaking as a learning opportunity, one which will improve your personal and professional life

- Accept that nervousness is okay—as long as you manage it and don't let it manage you
- Define your speech's exigence—what prompted the speech
- Analyze the other factors associated with your exigence—who is your audience, what are their expectations and needs, what is your speaking environment like (classroom, assembly hall, in front of the camera…), what are your speech's time constraints, which resources would add value to your speech, and what attire you will wear
- Determine your speech's general purpose, specific purpose, and purpose statement; from there determine your speech's main body points, then
- Draft an outline of your speech (see sample outline in Chapter 4) and begin reviewing the outline *several* days before your speech
- When practicing your speech, break the speech down into sections—introduction, main body point 1 and 2, internal summaries and transition statements, and conclusion. Commit to knowing those sections (the more you know ahead of time means the greater the chance you will have eye contact and not read from your notes during your speech)

What To Do During The Speech

- Remember to control your breathing—this will help calm you down (and not hyperventalate)
- Maintain eye contact with the audience. If you are uncomfortable looking them directly in the eye, look at their foreheads. They won't notice and will appreciate the effort. Eventually, try to look them in the eye because you can pick up on nonverbal cues which could help you adjust your speech
- Break the audience into three sections (left, center, and right) and look at people evenly in those sections. By doing this, you will not feel pressure to dart your eyes everywhere to look at everybody and risk looking too nervous
- Balance your rate, pitch, and volume according to the exigence and audience
- Respect time limits
- Maintain appropriate posture and limit nervous gestures while incorporating strategic gestures

What To Do After The Speech

- Reflect on how well you delivered your speech—what can you do better in terms of your delivery for the next speech?
- Ask yourself: did I achieve my purpose statement?

- Ask yourself: did my audience understand my speech?
- Seek input from others on what you did well and what you can do to improve—take the information you can use and disregard "irrelevant" information
- Reflect on what you did successfully (perhaps great eye contact, great introduction…) and how you can continue that success
- Maintain a positive attitude toward speaking

View the above as a checklist and abide by the checklist for every speech. In time, the checklist will become second nature to you. However, as you progress and advance in your speech making abilities you will probably be faced with more challenging situations. Chances are you will be called to give a persuasion speech or even a debate. Remember your fundamentals and believe in yourself. It is also recommended that you research elements of persuasion and debate in order to advance in these areas like you advanced through informative speeches. Below you will find resources that will enable you to have a better understanding of the persuasion and debate process.

Eagly, A.H., & Chaiken, S. (1993). *The psychology of attitudes*. Fort Worth, TX. Harcourt Brace Jovanovich.

Engel, S.M. (2000). *With good reason: An introduction to informal fallacies*. New York, NY. St. Martin's Press.

Kazoleas, D.C. (1993). A comparison of the persuasive effectiveness of qualitative versus quantitative evidence: A test of explanatory hypotheses. *Communication Quarterly*, *41*, 40-50.

Lucas, S. (2001). *The art of public speaking*. New York, NY. McGraw-Hill Higher Education.

Waddell, C. (1990). The role of pathos in the decision-making process: A study in the rhetoric of science policy. *Quarterly Journal of Speech*, *76*, 381-400.

Good luck to you as you move forward in the exciting and challenging area of public speaking. Remember, your success rests within you and your commitment to becoming a better speaker. It is ultimately your choice.

"It is common sense to take a method and try it. If it fails, admit it frankly and try another. But above all, try something."

Franklin D. Roosevelt

CHAPTER REFLECTION

1. Make a list of the new things you should be doing to become the effective public speaker you want to be (include time lines or dates of completion if necessary).

2. Make a list of the things you want to stop doing (those things which hinder your public speaking success, such as excessive "ums"), in order to become the effective public speaker you want to be (include time lines or dates of completion if necessary).

3. Make a list of the things you want to continue doing (i.e. those public speaking things you currently do well), in order to become the effective public speaker you want to be.

About the Author

Ryan is the Professional Development Coordinator and Department Chair of Academics at Antonelli College in Cincinnati, Ohio. In addition to studying human resource management, he has an M.A. and B.A. in Organizational Communication from Miami University (Ohio). Before arriving at Antonelli College, he worked in the management consulting industry researching and facilitating management development seminars for clients across the country and taught public speaking courses at Miami University (Ohio). His 2003 book *Creating A Home For Learning: The Art And Science Of Teaching: A Survival Guide To The Classroom*, also through 1stBooks, was co-authored with the Director of Education at Antonelli College, Jim Slouffman, and focuses on developing instructor effectiveness. Ryan resides in Cincinnati, Ohio with his wife Stephanie.

www.ingramcontent.com/pod-product-compliance
Lightning Source LLC
Chambersburg PA
CBHW030348290526
45785CB00004B/1651

* 9 7 8 1 4 1 0 7 6 0 4 4 9 *